Manuscripts of the Bible

GREEK BIBLES IN THE BRITISH LIBRARY

REVISED EDITION

T. S. PATTIE

THE BRITISH LIBRARY

Z
7771
. M3
P37
1995

© 1979 The British Library Board
Revised edition © 1995 The British Library Board
Published by
The British Library
Great Russell Street
London WC1B 3DG

British Library Cataloguing in Publication Data
A catalogue record for this title is available from
The British Library
ISBN 0-7123-0403-7
Designed by John Mitchell
Typeset in Linotype Bembo by Bexhill Phototypesetters
Printed in Great Britain by
Henry Ling Ltd, Dorchester

Why study ancient Bibles?

At the great councils of the church the Bible was solemnly brought in to symbolize the Bible's central position in the life of the Church. Originally the Orthodox liturgy began with the bringing in of the Gospels, and in the same way the Beadle carries the Bible into a Presbyterian church before leading the Minister in to start the service. The Jews also took very great care of their sacred books, and when any books were worn out they did not throw them away but locked them in a store called the Genizah. As the Bible is so important to Christianity we must be sure that it has been copied correctly and yet it is very difficult to copy exactly as anyone who has done any proof-reading will know. If you catch the 'Society for the Promotion of Cruelty to Children' before your book is printed, you can laugh at it. If it escapes the proof-reader's notice you will be embarassed, but the reader of your book will not be deceived, and may not even notice the error. If we make a systematic collection of errors in copying, we can use what we have learnt to reconstruct earlier stages of a text's history and go back to the 'archetype', or manuscript we think must have existed at the beginning.

The authority of the text of the Bible is soundly based. We now know and can list about 5,000 manuscripts of the Greek New Testament or parts of it and a smaller number of manuscripts of the Greek Old Testament. Of these only a dozen or so have the complete Bible, and these include three of the earliest, the fourth-century Codex Vaticanus and Codex Sinaiticus and the fifth-century Codex Alexandrinus. The second and third are now permanently exhibited in the British Library, which has one of the great collections of the world with its two hundred Greek New Testament manuscripts. The Sinaiticus and Vaticanus were written at the time when the whole Bible was collected in one volume for the first time. Before that the books of the Bible circulated separately, at first in scrolls,

1 *Gospels with 'Jerusalem Colophon'*, AD 1338.
Additional MS 5468, f.79. 226 leaves, 8¾×6¼ins (222×159mm). Greg. 686

and then in codex form, that is the familiar sewn book. It seems to have been the Christians who adopted and spread the use of the codex, which has not changed essentially until the rise of the paperback. At first the books of the Bible were written on papyrus, but the change to vellum (skin) did not materially affect its design which was taken over without change for printing.

The need for authority was felt at an early date, as we see in a note in that part of the Codex Sinaiticus which is in Leipzig. A corrector has written at the end of 2 Esdras (i.e. our Ezra and Nehemiah together) and Esther 'Collated with a very ancient manuscript of 1 Samuel to Esther corrected by the holy martyr Pamphilus.' The corrector goes on to say: 'At the end there is an autograph note by the same martyr: "The confessor

Antoninus compared it against the Hexapla of Origen and I, Pamphilus, corrected it in prison. It is not easy to find a copy the like of this one."' Pamphilus and Antoninus were martyred at Caesarea in Palestine in 310 and 309 respectively. The Hexapla was a scholarly edition of the Old Testament in six columns (hence its name), with the Hebrew text in the first column, the Hebrew in Greek characters in the second, and four different Greek translations in the next four columns. The learned scholar Origen of Alexandria was impressed by the authoritative Hebrew text, and his Hexapla carried great weight in matters relating to the text of the Bible. He was born in 185. When he was 17, his father was martyred, and when he was 18 he was head of the Christian school for Catechumens in Alexandria. The need for authority is also shown in Fig. 1, which shows a note at the end of the Gospel of Matthew: 'Written and corrected from the ancient copies in Jerusalem in the holy mountain. Published five years after Christ's ascension.' The date given for Matthew's Gospel, about AD 35, seems to us too early. We should rather date it about 70 or 80. The note is repeated in shorter form after each of the other Gospels in this medium-sized manuscript (Additional MS 5468) which is dated AD 1338.

The New Testament was originally written down in Greek in the decades following the Crucifixion, traditionally dated to the year 30. Paul's letters to the new Christian communities were highly prized; the need to communicate the message to the civilized world compelled the early Christians to write down the Gospels in Greek, and the fall of Jerusalem in AD 70 acted as a spur to them. The earliest surviving manuscript, in the John Rylands Library in Manchester, is a scrap of the Gospel of John dated by the handwriting to about 125, close to the date of composition, which we deduce to be between 90 and 130. Complete books survive from about 200, and quotations from authors like Tertullian, the first Christian theologian to write in Latin, and Irenaeus, Bishop of Lyons, who both lived in the second century of the Christian era, prove that the Bible as we know it was circulating then.

The story of the Old Testament is different because it was originally written in Hebrew. In the third century BC there was a large colony of Jews in the metropolis of Alexandria. There, under the successors of Alexander the Great, the Jews flourished and forgot their Hebrew, and accordingly their Bible was translated into the Greek which they spoke. Legends arose about this translation: how 72 elders, six from each tribe of Israel, were locked in separate cells and miraculously emerged with identical translations. The earliest account, however, reports that special quarters were

5

provided on the island of Pharos, the site of the most famous lighthouse in antiquity, and the scholars collaborated in producing an agreed text. Subsequently an annual festival was held on the island to commemorate the translation. Only the first five books were translated at this period, the Books of the Law, which already had a secure position in the Jewish tradition. The first translation was known as the Septuagint from the Latin 'septuaginta' or seventy, from the number of translators, or in one account the number of days it took to produce the translation. The language is the Hellenistic Greek which the Jews learned to speak in Alexandria, coloured by a proper respect for the inspired word of God, which He gave His people in Hebrew. It was a close and serviceable rendering, not free from error, but not slavishly literal. The translators were quite prepared to render 'the sons of God' in Genesis by the more acceptable 'the angels of God', or 'Circumcise the foreskin of your heart' in Deuteronomy by 'Circumcise your hard-heartedness'. The name 'Septuagint' was applied to the rest of the Old Testament including the Apocrypha, as it was progressively translated into Greek, or originally composed in Greek as some of the later books were. Later translations followed to a greater or lesser degree the model of the first five books. Isaiah and the Psalms, being poetic books, show more mistakes in translation. The Septuagint version of the book of Daniel did not prove acceptable and was replaced, in every Greek manuscript except two, by a later translation. The elegant literary Greek of the preface of Ecclesiasticus, which was apparently translated in 132 BC, contrasts sharply with the Septuagint style of its contents. Those books composed in Greek in the first century before Christ show the characteristics of contemporary Greek literary style.

In the first and second centuries AD the Jews of Palestine prepared a definitive list, or canon, of the books admitted to their Bible. About a dozen of the books which had already been translated into Greek were excluded, as well as parts of Esther and Daniel. The books that were included were arranged in a different order, some chapters were transposed and verses placed in a different sequence, and there were many differences of wording, besides plain mistakes. The Christians, however, venerated the Septuagint as divinely inspired. It had now become the traditional Bible of the Church. The Latin Bible, especially the Old Latin Version, the translation made before the scholar Jerome made the revision known as the Vulgate, is a direct translation of the Septuagint, and even Jerome was unable to suppress those books which the Jews rejected. The rejected books are known as the Apocrypha, or the Deutero-canonical books, and in the

Authorized Version and modern translations like the New English Bible the Apocrypha are collected together in an appendix. The Apocryphal books however appear in their proper places in the Vulgate. We can find traces of the Septuagint in the Psalms in the Book of Common Prayer. If we look at Psalm 14 (Psalm 13 of the Septuagint and Vulgate which number the Psalms differently), we see three extra verses which are in the Septuagint but not in the standard Hebrew text. They do not appear in the Authorized Version either, but the Book of Common Prayer uses the older translation of Miles Coverdale, which goes back to the Vulgate and the Septuagint. The passage is given below:

÷Their throat is an open sepulchre,
÷with their tongues have they deceived,
÷the poison of asps is under their lips.
÷Their mouth is full of cursing and bitterness,
÷their feet are swift to shed blood.
÷Destruction and unhappiness is in their ways,
÷and the way of peace have they not known,
÷there is no fear of God before their eyes:

This passage is contained in the fourth-century Vaticanus and Sinaiticus. The fifth-century Alexandrinus omits it, revealing a revision in the direction of the Hebrew text. A sixth or seventh-century corrector of the Sinaiticus has put brackets round the passage, intending it to be deleted, but a further corrector has carefully removed the brackets, thus restoring the text to its original condition. Against this passage we have placed the 'obelus', a sign (÷) like our division sign. It was used by Origen in his Hexapla to indicate that a word or passage was in the Septuagint but not in the Hebrew, and he used a colon (:) to indicate the end.

Jewish dissatisfaction with the Septuagint translation encouraged Aquila, who was a native of Sinope on the Black Sea and a distant relative of the emperor Hadrian (117–138), to make a new translation of the Old Testament. He was a convert to Judaism and studied Hebrew under the erudite Rabbi Akiba. His was an extremely literal version of the official Hebrew text, which reproduced in Greek not only the sense, but also the idiom, grammar and even etymology of the Hebrew, sometimes at the expense of clarity. This tour de force was acclaimed by Jews throughout the world and respected by those few Christian scholars who knew the Hebrew Bible. Its great merit was that it could be used to translate back into Hebrew with absolute reliability, and readers could therefore be sure

2 *Gospels with rare text of the Lord's Prayer,* 11th cent.

Egerton MS 2610, f.184b. 297 leaves, 5¾×4½ins (146×114mm). Greg. 700

that God's words had suffered no corruption. To those who knew no Hebrew, however, this translation made awkward reading.

A few fragments of this translation have survived. Parts of 1 and 2 Kings and of Psalms 90–103 were discovered in the debris of the Genizah of the Cairo synagogue, and parts of the Psalms in the Milan fragment of Origen's Hexapla. In 1 Kings 20: 10–13 Alexandrinus shows a few changes from the Septuagint to harmonize with Aquila. One change that shows up in English is at verse 10, where the Authorized Version and Aquila have: 'And Ben-Hadad sent unto him, and said, The gods do so unto me, and more also, if the dust of Samaria shall suffice for handfuls for all the people that follow me.' The Septuagint has instead: 'And the son of Hader sent unto him, saying, God do so unto me and more also, if the dust of Samaria shall suffice for the foxes for all the people that follow me.' Here the Codex Alexandrinus agrees with Aquila in reading 'The gods' rather than 'God'. The Septuagint in reading 'foxes' for 'handfuls' has made a plain mistake or else it relies on a different Hebrew text. Some manuscripts, including Royal MS 1 D. ii, a thirteenth-century manuscript in the British Library, read 'handfuls', in agreement with Aquila, the Hebrew, and apparently at least one other translator.

In the New Testament, too, we can see changes made deliberately as a result of editorial activity. Take for example Luke 14: 5 'Which one of you, if his ass or his ox fall in a well, will hesitate to pull it out even on the Sabbath day?' which is what the Codex Sinaiticus and many others read. A number of manuscripts including the Codex Vaticanus, the Codex Alexandrinus and Egerton MS 2610 (Fig. 2), an 11th-century Gospel in the British Library, have 'his son or his ox', a more dificult reading. Two manuscripts, being in doubt, combine both and read 'his son or his ass or his ox'. Clearly the last reading is a combination of the first two and therefore is not original. The RSV 2nd edition reads 'his son or his ox': was it felt to be too absurd or too undignified and therefore changed to the more natural 'ass or ox'? Or was the more unusual and difficult reading just a mistake? If we accept 'son or ox' we must suppose that to a farmer a son was as valuable a piece of farm equipment as an ox, or else that Jesus was making fun of the Sabbath law. A more difficult reading, even if in general preferable to an easy reading, must still make sense.

One ninth-century manuscript of the Gospels in the British Library, Additional MS 33277 (Fig. 3), like Sinaiticus, reads at Luke 14: 5 the easy 'ass or ox' (in Greek: *onos e bous*). In the type of writing in which this manuscript is written it is easy to confuse the Greek letters 'n' and 'r'. This

μὴ ιοῶ μρ τοο· ὁ ρκ ἐ ρι ἐμωο · οἱ δὲ ἢ
ρα τε ο τὶ ωὁ δ ὁρ ιᾶ · ναὶ τοο ς ὁ τοο
ἱ ο τί απο ο προ φ ι τωο · ναὶ οἱ απο ο
τα μ μ ἐμοι ιο ας ἐ λι τοομ φ αρισαι
ον· ναὶ η ρ ὡ τη σαν αυτομ ναὶ ς πο
αυτο · τι ο τι νααπ ι ζ τος οὐ ὁ υ ναὶ
ο χς · ου τ ἠ λιας · ου το ο προ φ ι τὶ
απο τε ρι θι αυτοι ς οὐ ο ω ἀμ μ ιος χρ τος
χρ ω ναπ ι ζ ωο τρ ιν ὁ απι· μ σ τοο ο
ὑμ ωμ ο ζ η νι λε ρ· ομ ὑμ σ τοο ναι οι ὁ ω
τε · αυτο ο στιμ ὁ ο πι ο ω μου ἐρχ
μ ἐρο ο ὁ ς ἐ μ προ ο θ ἐμου· ἀ γο ν ε
οὐ ε γω ουν να ει μ ι ἀξι ος ἱ ρ αε ὑο ο ωα αυ
τουτομ ἱ μ ας ται τοο ἡ ποδ ἐμα τοο
τα υτα ε ν β ι θα ρια εα ε ρ ε μ ς ο ω ὁ ρ αμ
του ιο ρδ αρου · οπου ιωα νι ι ω α μ μ ι ο
ναπ ι ζ ωομ γε τι θα υρι ο

λε ε πω τομ ιν ερχ ο μ ε ν ο μ προο αυ
τομ ναι λ ε γ ι · ι δε ο αμ ι ο ο του
θυ ο αι ρ ω ν τ ἡ ν ἁ μα ρτι απ του ι ο

ε ν ἁλλω
ε ρμ ι θ α ρα ι α

mistake is just as easy for modern readers as it was for ancient readers, as we can see in the third edition of the United Bible Societies' *Greek New Testament*. There this manuscript is reported as reading not *onos e bous* (ass or ox), but *oros e bous* (boundary or ox? boundary-stone or ox?), which does not make sense. This sort of mistake is fairly common in the manuscripts, but not so common that we can afford to be proud of our superior skill. In this case if we did not have the manuscript, but had only a later copy which read *oros* when the reading was *onos*, we should think that the manuscript from which the copy was made was written in a script in which it was possible to confuse 'n' and 'r' – just the kind of writing of Additional MS 33277, in fact. So a mistake of this sort can be used as a clue which will tell us something about a manuscript that no longer exists.

There are some surprising differences between the Authorized Version and a modern version of the Lord's Prayer in the Gospel of Luke.

Luke 11: 2–4

Authorized Version	*Revised Standard Version*
Our Father which art in heaven	Father
Hallowed be thy name	Hallowed be thy name
Thy kingdom come	Thy kingdom come
Thy will be done, as in heaven, so on earth	
Give us day by day our daily bread	Give us each day our daily bread
And forgive us our sins	And forgive us our sins
For we also forgive everyone that is indebted to us	For we also forgive everyone who is indebted to us;
And lead us not into temptation	And lead us not into temptation.
But deliver us from evil.	

It is worth looking in some detail at what the manuscripts say about these differences. First come the oldest manuscripts, written in uncial script (a script in capitals, as in Sinaiticus and Alexandrinus, see Figs 4, 6, PLATES II, III), then those written in minuscules (a cursive or lower case script invented in the ninth century: e.g. Figs 2, 3, 9, 10), then the translations

3 *Gospels*, 9th cent.
Additional MS 33277, f.274b. 353 leaves, 6×4½ins (152×114mm). Greg. 892

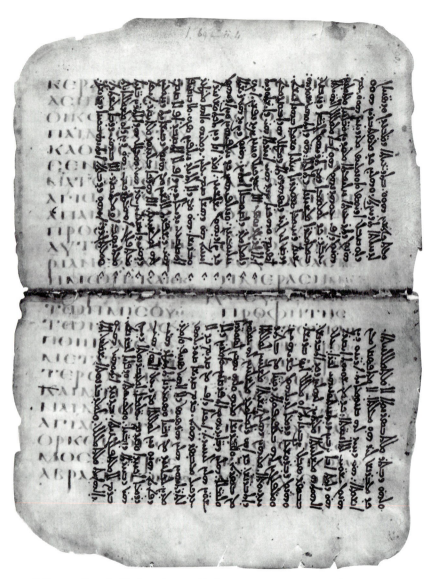

4 *Palimpsest Gospel of Luke*, 6th cent. Syriac upper text at right angles to the lower text, 8th–9th cent.

Additional MS 17211, f.5. 48 leaves, 12×9ins (305×229mm). Greg. 027

into other languages and lastly the quotations in the Church Fathers.

'Father': Codex Sinaiticus (ℵ), Codex Vaticanus (B), Bodmer Papyrus XIV–XV in Geneva, the minuscules numbered 1, 22, Egerton MS 2610 have 'Father' and so do the Armenian translation and the Vulgate (the Latin translation for which Jerome was responsible), as well as the quotation in the early Fathers Origen, Tertullian and Cyril, Patriarch of Alexandria (d. 444); one uncial manuscript in Paris (L) has 'Our Father'; Codex Alexandrinus (A), many uncials (including D) and minuscules and the Old Latin (pre-Jerome) translation and the Authorized Version all have 'Our Father in heaven'.

'Thy kingdom come':
Codex Bezae (D) at Cambridge, a bilingual Greek and Latin book of the Gospels Matthew, John, Luke, Mark, Acts in that order, written in the 5th century, has 'Thy kingdom come upon us'. Egerton MS 2610 has the extraordinary reading, presumably introduced from public worship in church: 'Thy holy spirit come upon us and cleanse us'. This reading is supported by a quotation from the works of the second-century heretic Marcion and from Saint Gregory of Nyssa in Cappadocia (d. 394). All the other manuscripts have the familiar reading.

'Thy kingdom come'
Bodmer Papyrus XIV–XV, B, L, 1, the group of manuscripts known as 'family 13', 22, the Armenian and Latin Vulgate translations as well as the texts used by Origen, Cyril, Tertullian and St Augustine, Bishop of Hippo, stopped here; Sinaiticus, Alexandrinus, D, and most manuscripts add 'Thy will be done on earth as in heaven'. This phrase, which the Authorized Version also gives, was probably introduced here because of the parallel passage in Matthew.

'And lead us not into temptation':
Bodmer Papyrus XIV–XV, Sinaiticus, B, L, 1 and its 'family', 22, Egerton MS 2610, the Armenian, Coptic and Latin Vulgate translations, Origen, Cyril, Tertullian and Augustine stop here; Alexandrinus, D, most Greek manuscripts, the 'Old Latin', Syriac and Ethiopian translations and the Authorized Version all have in addition 'But deliver us from evil'.

5 *Gospels with sections and table numbers*, 10th cent.
Additional MS 28815, f.135. 302 leaves, 11½×8ins (292×203mm). Greg. 699

Here we can see two of the principles adopted by textual critics: the earliest manuscripts are more valuable than the later ones and the shorter text is preferable to the longer text. Of course no manuscript has a monopoly of truth, or of good readings. Here Sinaiticus has 'Thy will be done on earth as in heaven', which is the longer (and therefore later) reading. At Luke 10: 41, 42 where Jesus says to Martha (in the New English Bible) 'you are fretting and fussing about so many things; but one thing is necessary' Sinaiticus and Vaticanus read instead of 'one thing is necessary' 'few things are necessary, or rather one alone' which gives itself away as a combination of two alternative readings. One manuscript has the other reading 'few things are necessary'. The longer reading is correct at Luke 12: 11: 'Take ye no thought how or what thing ye shall answer or what ye shall say.' Some witnesses, including D, have 'how ye shall answer' and other witnesses have 'what ye shall answer'.

The object of this detailed study of the text is to find out if possible what the author actually wrote. We assume of course that what he wrote made sense, and we have to bear in mind the possibility that no manuscript has the correct text. The phrase 'Sinai is a mountain in Arabia' at Galatians 4: 25 is a good example. Daniel Mace, a Presbyterian minister at Newbury, produced an edition of the New Testament in Greek and English in 1729. Although all the manuscripts have this phrase, Mace was independent enough to leave it out of his text, making the comment: 'This has all the marks of an interpolation: it is quite foreign to the argument, and serves only to perplex the apostle's reasoning, which without it appears very clear and coherent.' He rejects the argument that all the manuscripts without exception include this phrase with the contemptuous remark 'as if there was any manuscript so old as COMMON SENSE' (quoted in B. M. Metzger, *The Text of the New Testament,* 1968, p. 111). A similar marginal gloss is seen at Matthew 17: 24–27 in a tenth-century Gospels in the British Library (Additional MS 28815, f.26b) in which against 'two-drachma coin' (translated 'tribute-money' in the Authorized Version and 'temple-tax' in the New English Bible) there is a note 'two drachmas: 1½ nomismas' and, below, the 'stater' (the coin in the fish's mouth) is glossed '3 nomismas', a nomisma being a current Byzantine coin. The coin in the fish's mouth is therefore enough to pay the temple-tax of both Jesus and Peter. Daniel Mace supposed, quite reasonably, that in the same way 'Sinai is a mountain in Arabia' once stood in the margin and not in the text, but that a scribe incorporated it into the text by mistake.

The Codex Sinaiticus

THE CODEX SINAITICUS IS A JEWEL beyond price. It is named after the monastery of St Catherine in Sinai, where it was found. It is a large manuscript and though it has lost over 300 leaves from the Old Testament, it is still the earliest complete New Testament, and is the earliest and best witness for some of the books of the Old Testament. It dates from the triumph of Christianity, from the reign of Constantine the Great or one of his successors. Ironically it came into the possession of the atheistic USSR which, in desperate need of foreign currency, sold this inestimable Bible to the British Government in 1933 for £100,000, a sum comparable in magnitude, allowing for inflation, with the £1,763,000 raised in 1971 by the National Gallery to acquire Titian's *Death of Actaeon*. The acquisition of the manuscript aroused great interest and excitement, and over £53,000 was raised by public subscription, so that the British Government, which had promised to pay half, contributed in the end little more than £39,000.

The manuscript itself was first identified by Constantine Tischendorf, a German biblical scholar and tireless traveller in search of manuscripts. As he says himself in his *Codex Sinaiticus*, p. 23, 8th edition, London, [1934]:

It was at the foot of Mount Sinai, in the Convent of St Catherine, that I discovered the pearl of all my researches. In visiting the library of the monastery, in the month of May 1844, I perceived in the middle of the great hall a large and wide basket full of old parchments; and the librarian, who was a man of information, told me that two heaps of papers like these, mouldered by time, had been already committed to

6 *Codex Sinaiticus*, 4th cent. Altered ending to the Gospel of John.
Additional MS 43725, f.260. 390 leaves, 15×13ins (381×330mm)
Greg. 01 (ℵ)

ΣΚΖ Θ ΛΕΓΕΙΑΥΤΩ·ΝΑΙ
ΚΕΣΥΟΙΔΑΣΟΤΙ
ΦΙΛΩΣΕ·ΛΕΓΕΙΑΥ
ΤΩΒΟΣΚΕΤΑΑΡΝΙ
ΣΚΗ Ι ΑΜΟΥ·ΠΑΛΙΝΛΕ
ΓΕΙΑΥΤΩΣΙΜΩΝ
ΙΩΑΝΝΟΥ·ΑΓΑΠΑΣ
ΣΚΘ Θ ΜΕ·ΛΕΓΕΙΑΥΤΩΝΑΙ
ΚΕΣΥΟΙΔΑΣΟΤΙ
ΦΙΛΩΣΕ·ΛΕΓΕΙΑΥ
ΤΩΠΟΙΜΑΙΝΕΤΑ
ΣΛ Ι ΠΡΟΒΑΤΑΜΟΥ·ΛΕ
ΓΕΙΑΥΤΩΤΟΤΡΙΤΟΝ
ΣΙΜΩΝΙΩΑΝΝΟΥ
ΦΙΛΕΙΣΜΕ·ΕΛΥΠΗ
ΘΗΔΕΟΠΕΤΡΟΣΟ
ΤΙΕΙΠΕΝΑΥΤΩΤΟ
ΤΡΙΤΟΝΚΑΙΦΙΛΕΙΣ
ΜΕ·ΚΑΙΛΕΓΕΙΑΥ
ΤΩ·ΚΕΠΑΝΤΑΣΥΟΙ
ΔΑΣΣΥΓΙΝΩΣΚΕΙΣ
ΟΤΙΦΙΛΩΣΕΚΑΙ
ΣΛΑ Θ ΛΕΓΕΙΑΥΤΩΒΟΣΚΕ
ΤΑΠΡΟΒΑΤΑΜΟΥ·
ΑΜΗΝΑΜΗΝΛΕΓΩ
ΣΛΒ Β ΣΟΙΟΤΕΗΣΝΕΩ
ΤΕΡΟΣΕΖΩΝΝΥ
ΕΣΣΕΑΥΤΟΝ·ΚΑΙΠΕ
ΡΙΕΠΑΤΕΙΣΟΠΟΥΗ
ΘΕΛΕΣΟΤΑΝΔΕΓΗ
ΡΑΣΗΣΕΚΤΕΝΙΣΤΑΣ
ΧΙΡΑΣΣΟΥ·ΚΑΙΑΛ
ΛΟΙΖΩΣΟΥΣΙΝΣΕ
ΚΑΙΠΟΙΗΣΟΥΣΙΝ
ΣΟΙΟΣΑΟΥΘΕΛΙΣ·
ΤΟΥΤΟΔΕΕΙΠΕΝΣΗ
ΜΑΙΝΩΝΠΟΙΩ
ΘΑΝΑΤΩΔΟΞΑΣΕΙ
ΤΟΝΘΝ·ΚΑΙΤΟΥΤΟ
ΕΙΠΩΝΛΕΓΕΙΑΥ
ΤΩΑΚΟΛΟΥΘΙΜΟΙ
ΕΠΙΣΤΡΑΦΕΙΣΔΕ
ΟΠΕΤΡΟΣΒΛΕΠΕΙΤΟΝ
ΜΑΘΗΤΗΝΟΝΗΓΑ
ΠΑΟΙΣΚΑΙΑΝΕΠΙ
ΣΛΓ ΣΕΝΕΝΤΩΔΕΙΠΝΩ
ΕΠΙΤΟΣΤΗΘΟΣΑΥ

ΚΕΤΙΣΕΣΤΙΝΟΠΑ
ΡΑΔΙΔΟΥΣΣΕΤΟΥΤΟΝ
ΟΥΝΙΔΩΝΟΠΕΤΡΟΣ
ΕΙΠΕΝΤΩΙΥ·ΟΥΤΟΣΔΕ
ΤΙ·ΛΕΓΕΙΑΥΤΩ
ΟΙΣΕΑΝΑΥΤΟΝΘΕ
ΛΩΜΕΝΙΝΕΩΣΕΡ
ΧΟΜΑΙΤΙΠΡΟΣΣΕ·
ΣΥΜΟΙΑΚΟΛΟΥΘΙ·
ΕΞΗΛΘΕΝΟΥΝΟΥ
ΤΟΣΟΛΟΓΟΣΕΙΣΤΟΥΣ
ΑΔΕΛΦΟΥΣΟΤΙΟ
ΜΑΘΗΤΗΣΕΚΕΙ
ΝΟΣΟΥΚΑΠΟΘΝΗ
ΣΚΕΙ·ΟΥΚΕΙΠΕΝΔΕ
ΑΥΤΩΟΙΣΟΤΙΟΥΚΑ
ΠΟΘΝΗΣΚΕΙ·ΑΛΛ
ΑΝΑΥΤΟΝΘΕΛΩ
ΜΕΝΕΙΝΕΩΣΕΡΧΟ
ΜΑΙ·ΟΥΤΟΣΕΣΤΙΝ
ΜΑΘΗΤΗΣΟΜΑΡΤΥ
ΡΩΝΠΕΡΙΤΟΥΤΩΝ
ΚΑΙΓΡΑΨΑΣΤΑΥΤΑ
ΚΑΙΟΙΔΑΜΕΝΟΤΙ
ΑΛΗΘΗΣΕΣΤΙΝΗ
ΜΑΡΤΥΡΙΑΑΥΤΟΥ·
ΕΣΤΙΝΔΕΚΑΙΑΛΛΑ
ΠΟΛΛΑΑΕΠΟΙΗΣΕΝ
ΟΙΣΑΤΙΝΑΕΑΝΓΡΑ
ΦΗΤΑΙΚΑΘΕΝΟΥ
ΔΑΥΤΟΝΟΙΜΑΙΤΟΝ
ΚΟΣΜΟΝΧΩΡΗΣΕΙ
ΤΑΓΡΑΦΟΜΕΝΑΒΙ
ΒΛΙΑ:

ΕΥΑΓΓΕΛΙΟΝ

ΚΑΤΑ

ΙΩΑΝΝΗΝ

the flames. What was my surprise to find amid this heap of papers a considerable number of sheets of a copy of the Old Testament in Greek, which seemed to me to be one of the most ancient that I had ever seen. The authorities of the convent allowed me to possess myself of a third of these parchments, or about forty-three sheets, all the more readily as they were destined for the fire. But I could not get them to yield up possession of the remainder. The too lively satisfaction which I had displayed had aroused their suspicions as to the value of this manuscript.

The picture of the leaves of the Codex Sinaiticus lying in a basket about to be burned receives some general confirmation by a report by V. N. Beneshevich, a Russian biblical scholar, that he had heard from the steward Polycarp in 1908: 'Quite recently, in order to get rid of "rubbish", they heated the bread oven with old books, among which were very rare editions.'

Tischendorf took back to Frederick Augustus II of Saxony, who had sponsored his journey, the manuscripts he had collected including the 43 leaves from Sinai which he called the Codex Friderico-Augustanus in honour of his patron.

All these manuscripts were deposited in the University Library, Leipzig, where they still are. A second visit in 1853 brought to light eleven lines of Genesis, now in Leningrad. He came to the monastery for the third time on 31 January 1859. On 4 February the steward entertained him in his cell and, resuming a former conversation, said (p. 27 of the same book): 'And I too have read a Septuagint' (i.e. Greek Old Testament). He then brought out a 'bulky kind of volume, wrapped up in a red cloth and laid it before me. I unrolled the cover, and discovered, to my great surprise not only those very fragments which, fifteen years before, I had taken out of the basket, but also other parts of the Old Testament, the New Testament complete, and in addition the Epistle of Barnabas and a part of the Pastor of Hermas. Full of joy, which this time I had the self-command to conceal from the steward and the rest of the community, I asked, as if in a careless way, for permission to take the manuscript into my sleeping chamber to look over it more at leisure. There by myself I could give way to the transport of joy which I felt. I knew that I held in my hand the most precious Biblical treasure in existence – a document whose age and importance exceeded that of all the manuscripts which I had ever examined during twenty years' study of the subject.'

7 St Katherine's Monastery with gebel Musa in the background.
Ordnance Survey of the Peninsula of Sinai 1869.

Tischendorf borrowed the manuscript and presented it to the Emperor
of Russia, believing in his excitement that he had the monks' permission
to do so. It is possible that Tischendorf and the head of the monastery,
Cyril, Archbishop-Elect of Sinai, had a private agreement to this effect,
but when the proposal came to the ears of Cyril's enemies he was forced
in self-defence to say that there was no intention of giving away the
manuscript. This impossible situation was regularized by the Russian
diplomatic service ten years later, in 1869, by an agreement with the new

ΗΝΟΙΓΕΝΗΜΙΝΤΑΣΓΡΑΦΑΣ
ΚΑΙΑΝΑΣΤΑΝΤΕΣΑΥΤΗΤΗΩΡΑ
ΥΠΕΣΤΡΕΨΑΝΕΙΣΙΛΗΜΚΑΙΕΥ
ΡΟΝΗΘΡΟΙΣΜΕΝΟΥΣΤΟΥΣ
ΕΝΔΕΚΑΚΑΙΤΟΥΣΣΥΝΑΥΤΟΙΣ
ΛΕΓΟΝΤΑΣΟΤΙΗΓΕΡΘΗΟΚΣ
ΤΟΣ ΚΑΙΩΦΘΗΣΙΜΩΝΙ ΚΑΙ
ΑΥΤΟΙΕΞΗΓΟΥΝΤΟΤΑΕΝΤΗ
ΚΑΙΩΦΘΗΓΝΩΣΘΗΑΥΤΟΙΣΕΝ
ΤΗΚΛΑΣΕΙΤΟΥΑΡΤΟΥ
ΤΑΥΤΑΔΕΑΥΤΩΝΛΑΛΟΥΝΤΩΝ
ΑΥΤΟΣΟΙΣΕΣΤΗΕΜΜΕΣΩΑΥ
ΤΩΝ ΚΑΙΛΕΓΕΙΑΥΤΟΙΣΕΙΡΗ
ΥΜΙΝ ΠΤΟΗΘΕΝΤΕΣΔΕΚΑΙ
ΕΜΦΟΒΟΙΓΕΝΟΜΕΝΟΙΕΔΟ
ΚΟΥΝΠΝΑΘΕΩΡΕΙΝΚΑΙΕΙΠΕ
ΑΥΤΟΙΣ ΤΙΤΕΤΑΡΑΓΜΕΝΟΙΕ
ΕΣΤΑΙΚΑΙΔΙΑΤΙΔΙΑΛΟΓΙΣΜΟΙ
ΑΝΑΒΑΙΝΟΥΣΙΝΕΝΤΑΙΣΚΑΡ
ΔΙΑΙΣΥΜΩΝ ΕΙΔΕΤΑΣΧΕΙ
ΡΑΣΜΟΥΚΑΙΤΟΥΣΠΟΔΑΣΜΟΥ
ΟΤΙΑΥΤΟΣΕΓΩΕΙΜΙ ΨΗΛΑΦΗ
ΣΑΤΕΜΕΚΑΙΙΔΕΤΕ ΟΤΙΠΝΑ
ΣΑΡΚΑΚΑΙΟΣΤΕΑΟΥΚΕΧΕΙ
ΚΑΘΩΣΕΜΕΘΕΩΡΕΙΤΕΕΧΟΝΤΑ
ΚΑΙΤΟΥΤΟΕΙΠΩΝΕΠΕΔΕΙΞΕ
ΑΥΤΟΙΣΤΑΣΧΕΙΡΑΣΚΑΙΤΟΥ
ΠΟΔΑΣ ΕΤΙΔΕΑΠΙΣΤΟΥΝ
ΤΩΝΑΥΤΩΝΑΠΟΤΗΣΧΑΡΑΣ
ΚΑΙΘΑΥΜΑΖΟΝΤΩΝΕΙΠΕΝΑΥΤΟΙ
ΕΧΕΤΕΤΙΒΡΩΣΙΜΟΝΕΝΘΑΔΕ
ΟΙΔΕΕΠΕΔΩΚΑΝΑΥΤΩΙΧΘΥΟ
ΟΠΤΟΥΜΕΡΟΣΚΑΙΑΠΟΛΟΜΙ
ΕΝΑΠΙΟΝΑΥΤΩΝ
ΕΙΠΕΝΔΕΑΥΤΟΙΣΟΥΤΟΙΟΙΛΟΓΟ
ΜΟΥΟΥΣΕΛΑΛΗΣΑΠΡΟΣΥΜΑΣ
ΕΤΙΩΝΣΥΝΥΜΙΝΟΤΙΔΕΙ
ΠΛΗΡΩΘΗΝΑΙΠΑΝΤΑΤΑΓΕ
ΓΡΑΜΜΕΝΑΕΝΤΩΝΟΜΩ
ΜΩΣΕΩΣΚΑΙΠΡΟΦΗΤΑΙΣ
ΚΑΙΨΑΛΜΟΙΣΠΕΡΙΕΜΟΥ
ΤΟΤΕΔΙΗΝΟΙΞΕΝΑΥΤΩΝΤΟ
ΝΟΥΝΤΟΥΣΥΝΙΕΝΑΙΤΑΣΓΡΑ
ΦΑΣ ΚΑΙΕΙΠΕΝΑΥΤΟΙΣΟΤΙ
ΟΥΤΩΣΓΕΓΡΑΠΤΑΙΠΑΘΕΙΝΤΟ
ΧΝΚΑΙΑΝΑΣΤΗΝΑΙΕΚΝΕΚΡΩ
ΤΗΤΡΙΤΗΗΜΕΡΑ ΚΑΙΚΗΡΥ
ΧΘΗΝΑΙΕΠΙΤΩΟΝΟΜΑΤΙΑΥ
ΤΟΥΜΕΤΑΝΟΙΑΝΚΑΙΑΦΕ
ΣΙΝΑΜΑΡΤΙΩΝΕΙΣΠΑΝΤΑ

ΤΑΕΘΝΗ ΑΡΞΑΜΕΝΟΝΑΠΟΙ
ΙΛΗΜ ΥΜΕΙΣΔΕΕΣΤΑΙΜΑΡΤΥ
ΡΕΣΤΟΥΤΩΝ ΚΑΙΙΔΟΥΕΓΩ
ΑΠΟΣΤΕΛΛΩΤΗΝΕΠΑΓΓΕΛΙΑ
ΤΟΥΠΡΣΜΟΥΕΦΥΜΑΣ ΥΜΕΙΣ
ΔΕΚΑΘΙΣΑΤΕΕΝΤΗΠΟΛΕΙ
ΕΩΣΟΥΕΝΔΥΣΗΣΘΑΙΔΥΝΑΜΙ
ΜΙΝΕΞΥΨΟΥΣ ΕΞΗΓΑΓΕΝΔΕ
ΑΥΤΟΥΣΕΞΩΕΩΣΕΙΣΒΗΘΑΝΙΑ
ΚΑΙΕΠΑΡΑΣΤΑΣΧΕΙΡΑΣΑΥΤΟΥ
ΕΥΛΟΓΗΣΕΝΑΥΤΟΥΣ
ΚΑΙΕΓΕΝΕΤΟΕΝΤΩΕΥΛΟΓΙ
ΑΥΤΟΝΑΥΤΟΥΣΔΙΕΣΤΗΑΠ
ΤΩΙΚΑΙΑΝΕΦΕΡΕΤΟΕΙΣΤΟΝ
ΟΥΝΟΝ ΚΑΙΑΥΤΟΙΠΡΟΣΚΥΝΗ
ΣΑΝΤΕΣΑΥΤΟΝΥΠΕΣΤΡΕ
ΕΙΣΙΛΗΜΜΕΤΑΧΑΡΑΣΜΕΓΑΛΗΣ
ΚΑΙΗΣΑΝΔΙΑΠΑΝΤΟΣΕΝΤ
ΤΕΡΕΣΚΑΙΕΥΛΟΓΟΥΝΤΕΣΤΟ
ΘΝΑΜΗΝ

ΕΥΑΓΓΕΛΙΟΝ ΚΑΤΑ ΛΟΥΚΑΝ

Archbishop of Sinai, Callistus, in which the monks agreed to donate the manuscript to the Emperor, and the Emperor gave the monks some money and some decorations. However, the monks on Sinai still resent the way in which their treasure was given away.

Once the manuscript was in St Petersburg Tischendorf gave it the name of Codex Sinaiticus Petropolitanus, in honour of its place of discovery and its place of residence. He prepared a luxurious edition complete with scholarly commentary, printed in 'facsimile type', of the 346½ leaves, which was published in 1862 at Russian expense. The 43 leaves at Leipzig he had already published. Both parts were published in 1911–1922 in collotype facsimile by Kirsopp and Helen Lake.

The text of our Bible is supremely well attested, but there are a few puzzles. One of these is the ending of the Gospel of Mark, which has two main forms, the long ending and the short ending. The Sinaiticus agrees with other early manuscripts like the Vaticanus in having the short ending. Another puzzle is the story of the woman taken in adultery (John 7: 58–8: 11) which some manuscripts place after John 7: 36, or 7: 52, or 21: 24, or even after Luke 21: 38. The Sinaiticus, like the Vaticanus, omits the adulterous woman altogether. Are we to assume that at an early date an unknown editor decided to leave out both of these sections, this decision being reflected in the Sinaiticus and Vaticanus, but not in the text which became standard in the Orthodox Church and thence in the Authorized Version? It seems quite likely. There is no separate translation of the Codex Sinaiticus, but many of its readings, including the two we have just discussed, are recorded in the *New English Bible*, and in 1869 Tischendorf published in Leipzig an edition of the English Authorized Version, with the variant readings in English of the Sinaiticus, Vaticanus, and Alexandrinus as the thousandth volume in the Tauchnitz collection of British authors.

But was any ancient Bible really worth £100,000? Had the orange not been squeezed dry by Tischendorf and Professor Lake? H. J. M. Milne and T. C. Skeat, of the Department of Manuscripts of the British Museum, showed in their book *Scribes and Correctors of the Codex Sinaiticus*, which was published in 1938, how much more there was still to be discovered.

Plate II *Codex Alexandrinus*, 5th cent. Colophon of Luke.
Royal MS 1 D. viii, f.41b. 772 leaves, 12½×10ins (317×254mm). Greg. 02 (A)

Milne and Skeat were able to show decisively that only three scribes and not four were responsible for the manuscript (Tischendorf had called the anonymous scribes A, B, C, and D: but the work attributed to C should in reality be attributed to A and D). These three scribes, who were all carefully trained to write in the same style, can be distinguished not so much by the letter forms, as by the general appearance of the page, some habits of punctuation, and above all the decorative tail-piece with which the scribe ended each book of the Bible. The tail-piece amounts to the scribe's signature and Milne and Skeat were able to show that the tail-piece could be used to distinguish scribes in the other two early Greek Bibles, Codex Vaticanus and Codex Alexandrinus.

After the scribes of the Codex Sinaiticus had been securely identified, an interesting feature emerged – they were not equally good at spelling. Greek spelling is like English in that both became fixed at a certain period, but the pronunciation changed in succeeding centuries. Consequently Greek speakers of the period after Christ, like English speakers of today, had to learn correct spelling by memory. Of the three scribes, D was an excellent speller, A a poor speller, and B an appallingly bad speller. It is an entertaining thought that the human frailty of the weakest of these spellers is enough to demolish a theory formulated sixteen hundred years later. The traditional view was that commercial copies of books were made by a group of scribes listening to a reader. However in 1928 Kurt Ohly put forward the theory in his *Stichometrische Untersuchungen* that dictation was not used, and pointed to the marks indicating the number of lines written (stichometry) and to the consideration that a certain number of scribes copying and recopying by eye would produce the same amount of work as if dictation were used, and of course far more accurately. Ohly's theory is exploded by the evidence of spelling – the miserable scribe B omits letters or syllables or duplicates syllables or adds meaningless letters in a way that would be incredible if he were copying by eye. Besides, Maccabees and Psalms are both begun by D and continued by A, and the spelling reflects the change of hand. From another point of view B's spelling is valuable evidence of the current pronunciation, which was more like modern than ancient Greek, such as the confusion between οι and υ, and omission of intervocalic γ (ηνυγην for ἠνοίγην, φευων for φεύγων and conversely λεγοντες for λέοντες). It is worth making the point that there were other scribes who could spell as well as D.

Under ultra-violet light it is possible to read letters that have been erased and written over. Using this technique it was discovered that originally the

Gospel of John ended at 21: 24. The tail-piece and end-title were later deleted, and verse 25 was added with a fresh tail piece and end-title (Fig. 7). It seemed that an unknown editor decided on internal grounds that the Gospel ended at 21: 24, and that verse 25 was an interpolation, which has been argued in modern times.

Another surprise was at Matthew 6: 28: 'Consider how the lilies grow in the fields; they do not work, they do not spin.' This is the reading of the *New English Bible* which also adds at the foot of the page: 'One witness reads "Consider the lilies: they neither card nor spin nor labour"'. This is the original reading of the Codex Sinaiticus, subsequently corrected to the familiar version. The original reading, detected with the aid of ultra-violet light, seems a great improvement on the familiar reading, and it makes a perfect parallel with the birds of the air in verse 26: 'they do not sow and reap and store in barns.'

Plate III *Purple Gospels*, 6th cent.
Cotton MS Titus C. xv, f.2b. 4 leaves, 12¾×10½ins (324×267mm). Greg. 022 (N)

The Codex Alexandrinus

THIS ANCIENT BIBLE, NAMED AFTER THE capital of Greek Egypt, famous for its scholarship and research, was written in the first half of the fifth century, slightly later than the other two great Greek codices of the bible, Vaticanus and Sinaiticus. It contains the complete Bible (including the Apocrypha) except for nine leaves in the Psalms, the first twenty-five leaves of Matthew, and a few other leaves, and it contains in addition almost all of the two Letters of Clement, Bishop of Rome about AD 96, and the Canticles or Odes, i.e. the passages of Scripture which are sung as hymns, such as the Magnificat and the Nunc Dimittis. Vaticanus and Sinaiticus do not have the Canticles. The manuscript consists of 773 large leaves, and once had about forty more. Two scribes, who differ in their handwriting, their spelling and the patterns of the decorative end-pieces which they added at the end of each book, were responsible for the production of the volume. The decorative end-title of Baruch, one of the Apocryphal books, is illustrated in plate II, the work of the first scribe. Where Sinaiticus was written in four columns except for the Psalms and the other poetical books, which were written in two columns, and the Vaticanus was written in three columns, the Alexandrinus was written throughout in two columns.

We must remember that the one-volume Bibles were made up of very small books that had previously circulated entirely separately, and that therefore we must expect their character to vary from book to book. In Deuteronomy and Revelation Alexandrinus has a good text, agreeing with the Deuteronomy at the John Rylands Library in Manchester which was written on papyrus six centuries earlier. On the other hand the text of the Gospels is well on the way to the Byzantine text and the Authorized Version. For the second and third books of the Maccabees it is our oldest witness.

It is not certain that the Codex Alexandrinus was originally written in

8 *Cyril Lucar* (1572–1638) Patriarch of Constantinople. Bibliothèque publique et universitaire, Geneva.

Photo: Christian Porte.

Alexandria, as its name suggests, despite the tradition that it was written by St Thecla, the legendary convert and companion of the Apostle Paul. A later St Thecla lived and was martyred in the 4th century, but even this is too early for our manuscript, despite Cyril Lucar's note of authentication. He says that the name of Thecla, once written at the end of the book, had disappeared through loss of leaves after the Mohammedan conquest of Egypt. We are on surer ground about AD 1300, for a note in Arabic at the foot of the first page of Genesis says: 'Bound to the Patriarchal Cell in the Fortress of Alexandria. Whoever removes it thence shall be excommunicated and cut off. Written by Athanasius the humble.' This is undoubtedly Athanasius II, Patriarch of Alexandria from 1276 to 1316, who is known to have brought manuscripts from Constantinople to the Patriarchal Library in Alexandria. It is therefore probable that he acquired the great Bible in Constantinople too. In 1627 it was given to Charles I of Great Britain by Cyril Lucar the calvinistical Patriarch of Constantinople 1620–1638, who had previously been Patriarch of Alexandria. It was originally offered in January 1625 to Sir Thomas Roe, British ambassador to the Sublime Porte, to be presented to James I, but that monarch died in March 1625, and the manuscript was not presented until the New Year of 1627, by which time Charles I had succeeded his father.

From 1627 until Charles I's execution on 30th January 1649, the Codex Alexandrinus, bound in four volumes, each with the Royal cypher, was kept at St James's Palace with the rest of the Royal Library. During the Commonwealth (1649–1660) troops were quartered in the palace, and the books were allowed to 'lie upon the floor in confused heaps, so that not only the rain and the dust, but also the rats, mice and other vermin can easily get at them' (*Calendar of State Papers Domestic 1651*, p. 468). Conditions were no better in 1693 when Richard Bentley, the brilliant classical scholar, famous for his daring corrections, was appointed Keeper of the Royal Library. He kept the great Bible in his own lodgings, so ashamed was he of the dilapidated state of the library room.

Early in the eighteenth century the Royal Library was moved to Cotton House, an 'Ancient Mansion House in Westminster', to join the valuable library of Sir Robert Cotton (1571–1631) which was settled upon an unappreciative nation in 1700. In Cotton House the books were kept in a damp, narrow little room, with only one window at each end. The arch over one of the windows was in a ruinous condition and ready to fall, as was also the arch upon which the room was built. Sir Christopher Wren was asked how best to improve Cotton House, and in his report (*Calendar*

Plate IV *Bristol Psalter*, 10th – 11th cent. David and the musicians.
Additional MS 40731, f.7b. 265 leaves, 4×3½ins (102×89mm)

Plate V *Bristol Psalter*, 10th – 11th cent. Isaiah between Night and Dawn (Canticle 5)
Additional MS 40731, f.252. 265 leaves, 4×3½ins (102×89mm)

of Treasury Books, 1702–1707, p. 476) he considered that the house was so ruinous that the only possible course was demolition of all or most of it. His opinion of the contents was unflattering: 'I confesse both these libraries may be purged of much useless trash, but this must be the drudgery of librarians.' His opinion was not acted upon, for Cotton House was not pulled down, nor were the libraries 'purged'.

But in 1722 Cotton House was in such an alarming condition that the two libraries were moved on a seven-year lease into Essex House, in Essex Street in the Strand. When the lease expired in 1729, the rent was too high, and the collections were moved to Ashburnham House, in Little Dean's Yard, which was considered 'much more safe from fire'. This move took place in 1730; but in the following year disaster struck. In the words of the *Report of the House of Commons Committee*, 9th May 1732: 'On Saturday morning, October 23, 1731, a great smoke was perceived by Dr Bentley and the rest of the family at Ashburnham House, which soon after broke out into a flame: *It began from a wooden mantel-tree taking fire which lay across a stove-chimney* that was under the room where the MSS of the Royal and Cottonian Libraries were lodged, and was communicated to that room by the wainscot and by pieces of timber, that stood perpendicularly upon each end of the mantel-tree. They were in hopes, at first, to put a stop to the fire by throwing water upon the pieces of timber and wainscot . . . and therefore did not begin to remove the books so soon as they otherwise would have done. But, the fire prevailing, Mr Casley, the Deputy-Librarian, took care in the first place to remove the famous *Alexandrian MS*, and the books under the head of Augustus (there was the bust of a Roman Emperor above twelve of the presses) in the Cottonian Library, as being esteemed the most valuable in the collection. Several entire presses, with the books in them, were also removed, but . . . several of the backs of the presses being already on fire, they were obliged to be broke open, and the books, as many as could be, thrown out of the windows.' An eye-witness tells of the learned Doctor Bentley in 'nightgown and great wig' stalking out of the building with the Codex Alexandrinus under his arm. Did Dr Bentley manage to carry all four volumes under his arm? Or just one? We do not know but we can be thankful that all four were saved. Arthur Onslow, Speaker of the House of Commons, and one of the Trustees of the Cotton Library, came across from his nearby residence to direct the rescue. When the cost was counted it became clear that the Royal Library had escaped lightly, but the Cotton Library had suffered severely. Of the 958 manuscripts in the Cotton Library, 114 were reckoned to be 'lost, burnt, or entirely spoiled', and a further 98 damaged. Mr Speaker Onslow was instrumental in arranging for the damaged manuscripts to be promptly repaired. After three months of energetic restoration, the Keeper of the Exchequer-Records was able to report his progress: 'One hundred and upwards, being volumes of Letters and State-Papers, have been quite taken to pieces, washed and bound again.' The disastrous fire may have drawn public attention to the plight of the Cotton and Royal Libraries. At any rate a generation later they were both in the newly founded British Museum, and in the next century Frederic Madden, the energetic and cantankerous Keeper of Manuscripts, was able to make many more repairs to the burnt Cottons.

The arrival of the Alexandrinus in Britain, sixteen years after the publication of the Authorized Version in 1611, gave a powerful stimulus towards the criticism of the text of the New Testament. It was the first of the three great codices to have its New Testament published. The Old Testament of the Codex Vaticanus, which has been in the Vatican Library at least since 1481, had already been made public in Pope Sixtus V's Septuagint of 1587; however its text of the New Testament was not published until after the Alexandrinus and the Sinaiticus were fully published. Patrick Young was the Royal Librarian when the new treasure arrived and his scholarly studies went far towards raising the reputation of the Royal Library. Young published the first printed edition of the Letters of Clement from the Alexandrian Bible in 1633. His preparatory work for an edition of the entire Bible was incorporated after his death in the London Polyglot Bible of 1657, which gave the text of the Bible in Hebrew, Greek, Ethiopic, Syriac and Arabic. In 1701–1720 a complete edition of the Old Testament was produced by John Ernest Grabe, a Prussian scholar who settled in Oxford. In his edition all deviations from the manuscript were distinguished by being printed in smaller type, the original reading being given in the margin. The New Testament was published in 1786, when an edition in uncial type specially cast for this purpose was produced by C. G. Woide (1725–1790), a native of Poland who in 1782 was appointed assistant librarian in the British Museum.

Plate VI *Eusebian Canon Tables*, 7th cent.
Additional MS 5111, f.11. 2 leaves, 8½×7ins (216×178mm)

Fragments of Uncial Manuscripts

ONE OF THE MANUSCRIPTS SEVERELY DAMAGED in the fire at Ashburnham House was the Cotton Genesis, a medium-sized fifth- or sixth-
century Greek Genesis with illustrations. Some of the leaves of this
manuscript were totally destroyed, and those that remain are shrunken and
distorted by the heat. Although the painting was not of as high quality as
the famous Vienna Genesis, so little manuscript painting of an early date
has survived that we bitterly lament its tragic loss. The Septuagint Genesis
is also represented in the British Library by a papyrus fragment of Chapter
5 in the Old Latin Version, which was directly translated from the Greek.
This Latin fragment, Papyrus 2052, was also written in uncials.

Fire is not the only hazard. A large and luxurious sixth-century manuscript of the four Gospels on purple vellum, written in silver (which has
oxidized to black) except for the contracted names of God and Jesus which
are written in gold, has been dismembered. It probably contained 462
leaves when it was first made, and we may suppose that it was written in
Constantinople, and taken apart in the twelfth century by Crusaders. At
any rate only 230 leaves survive, 182 in Leningrad, 33 in the Greek island
of Patmos, and the rest scattered throughout the world. PLATE III shows
one of the four leaves in the British Library (Cotton MS Titus C. xv, f.2b),
which contains Matthew 2: 61–65.

Another hazard which faces manuscripts is obsolescence. If a manuscript
was no longer used, its text could be erased and the vellum re-used for
another text. Such a twice-written manuscript is called 'palimpsest'.
Additional MSS 17210 and 17211 together form a treatise in Syriac by
Severus, patriarch of Antioch, against Johannes Grammaticus, written in
the eighth or ninth century. To make this manuscript 48 large leaves of
the Gospel of Luke, five leaves of Euclid, and 4,000 lines of Homer, all in
Greek and all of the sixth century, were erased. There was little use for

Greek manuscripts after the Arab conquest. These manuscripts with 500 others were bought through the Rev. Henry Tattam in three lots in 1841, 1843 and 1847 from the Syrian monastery of St Mary the Mother of God in the Nitrian Desert, 70 miles north-west of Cairo. The Nitrian Desert was once thickly populated by Christian monasteries. Fig. 4 (Additional MS 17211, f.5) contains Luke 1: 69–2: 4, written at right angles to the Syriac upper script.

It is surprising to find so many Syriac manuscripts in the Egyptian desert. This one was written by Simeon, a recluse in the monastery of Mar Simeon of Kartmin, for Daniel, who later became bishop of Edessa and bequeathed it on his death to the monastery of Mar Silas at Sarug. It was probably one of the 250 manuscripts brought in 932 by Moses of Nisibis to the monastery of Mary the Mother of God in the Nitrian desert.

Aids to Readers

TODAY IF WE WISH TO LOOK UP a reference in the Bible, we use the modern chapters and verses. Our system of chapters is attributed to Stephen Langton, Archbishop of Canterbury (1206–1228), and the verses were not applied to the New Testament until 1551. In ancient times people used to rely on their memories much more than nowadays, but there were times when they needed to check their references. So at least as early as the fourth century, the text was divided into chapters, but not the same chapters as the ones familiar to us. At the beginning of each book there was a list of the chapters with their titles. In addition there was in the Gospels a division into short sections. These sections were numbered, and a set of tables ('Canon Tables') in front of the Gospel of Matthew enabled readers to find parallel passages in the other Gospels, or to establish that there were none. The sections in the Gospels are usually attributed to a man called Ammonius, and the tables were invented or perfected by Eusebius of Caesarea in Palestine, the 'Father of Church History'. Similar sections in the book of Acts are attributed to a shadowy Euthalius. Two leaves of the Tables of Eusebius have survived from what was once a splendid medium-sized manuscript, written on gold in the seventh century (Additional MS 5111, ff. 10, 11). This manuscript may have been written in Constantinople itself. One page is illustrated (f. 11, PLATE VI). It contains Tables 8 (Correspondences between Matthew and Mark), 9 (Luke and John), and 10 (Matthew alone).

This remnant is particularly valuable because it is one of the few examples of illuminated manuscripts dating from before the period of the Iconoclast Emperors of the East (726–842), when it was forbidden to reproduce the human figure in church or Bible. In Table 8 we see that section 12 in Matthew corresponds to 23 in Mark, 14 to 25, 28 to 29 and so on. The Greeks used the first nine letters of their alphabet for the units

1 to 9, including ς, a form of F (vau), for 6, the next nine for the tens, including φ (qoppa) for 90, and the next nine for the hundreds, including λ (sanpi) for 900. This system incidentally was taken over by the Arab astronomers, who used letters equivalent to the Greek letters, in the order of the ancient Semitic alphabet.

Additional MS 11300 shows how the system worked. It contains the four gospels written in the tenth century on 268 small leaves. On f.26b, (Fig. 9) we can see in the upper margin, in blue ink, the titles of chapters 17 and 18 (IZ, IH): About the two Blind Men, and About the Dumb Man possessed by a Spirit (Matthew 9: 27 and 9: 32). In the left-hand margin the numbers 17 and 18, also in blue, are set against the beginning of the chapters. The section number, 75, is also set in the margin at verse 27, in black; immediately below it is the table-number, 10. Table 10, of Matthew alone, is illustrated in our plate of the Canon Tables (PLATE VI): 75 is in the second last column, sixteenth from the top, though somewhat indistinct. On the same page is marked the beginning of the Lesson from the Gospels for the sixth Sunday of the general series of Sundays with an introductory phrase: '6th Sunday: At that time when Jesus departed'.

Another page of the same manuscript f.31 (Fig. 10) shows two 'scholia', or marginal notes, at Matthew 11: 17

> We piped to you and you did not dance;
> we wailed, and you did not mourn.

'We piped' is marked with the sign $\varnothing$ and the corresponding note, which has the same mark, goes as follows: 'That is, We gave you the teaching of gladness and the kingdom of heaven and you did not receive it with joy.' 'We wailed' is marked with the 'asteriskos' ※, as is the corresponding note: 'Instead of, We threatened you with scowls and punishment and you did not repent of your sins'.

Many other manuscripts have the same aids for readers at this one, but few are so colourful. Additional MS 33277, a small fat ninth-century manuscript of the four Gospels written in minuscule script, also has the sections and table-numbers, and marks the beginnings and ends of the Gospel Lessons. Spaces have been left for the words 'Beginning' and 'End', although 'Beginning' is usually written in the margin, and sometimes these

9 *Gospels showing chapters, sections and lessons*, 10th cent.
Additional MS 11300, f.26b. 267 leaves, 7×4¾ins (178×121mm). Greg. 478

θον ἐξῆρὰπ ηος της χάρος ἀυτῆς.
καὶ λόγος θ̅ κ̅ τ̅οῖς ὁρασ ἰον · καὶ ἐ
ξῆλθεν ἡ φημὴ ἀυτη. εἰς ὅλην
τὴν γῆν ἐκείνην ·
ραγοντι ἐκεῖθεν τ̅ω̅ι̅υ̅ · ἠκολού
θησαν ἀυτῶ δύο τυφλοι. κρά
ζοντες · καὶ λέγοντες · ἐλέησον
ἡμᾶς υ̅ϲ̅ δα̅δ̅· ἐλθόντι δὲ ἐς
τὴν οἰκίαν. προσῆλθον ἀυτῶ
οἱ τυφλοι · καὶ λέγει ἀυτοῖς ὁ ι̅ϲ̅ ·
πιστεύετε ὅτι δύναμαι τοῦτο ποι
ῆσαι; λέγουσιν ἀυτῶ· ναὶ κ̅ε̅ ·
τότε ἥψατο τῶν ὀφθαλμῶν ἀυ
τῶν λέγων · κατὰ τὴν πίϲτιν
ὑμῶν γενηθήτω ὑμῖν · καὶ
ἀνεώχθησαν ἀυτῶν οἱ ὀφθαλ
μοι · καὶ ἐνεβριμήσατο ἀυτοῖς
ὁ ι̅ϲ̅ λέγων · ὁρᾶτε μηδεὶς γινω
σκέτω · οἱ δὲ ἐξελθόντες διε
φήμισαν ἀυτὸν. ὲν ὅλη τῆ γῆ
ἐκείνη · Ἀυτῶν δὲ ἐξερχο
μένων. ἰδού προσήνεγκαν
ἀυτῶ ἄνον κωφον δαιμονιζό
μενον · καὶ ἐκβληθέντος
τοῦ δαιμονίου. ἐλάλησεν ὁ
κωφος · καὶ ἐθαύμασαν οἱ ὄχλοι

gaps have not been filled, showing that this operation was carried out after the main text was written. One scholar observed that there were gaps at the foot of some pages and suggested that this was a direct copy of an older uncial manuscript, which the scribe was copying line for line and page for page, a very difficult task. But it is not the gaps that need to be explained – they have been left for 'Beginning' and 'End'. What is odd is that the scribe has written an extra half line at the foot of some pages and an extra line and a half at the foot of the second page. Perhaps he was copying page for page, but he may just have made a mistake in the first two pages and had to re-write them and stick them in afterwards. In the Gospels of Matthew, Luke and John this manuscript has the same sort of readings as the later Byzantine Text (i.e. like the Authorized Version), but in Mark it is much more nearly related to Sinaiticus than in the other three Gospels. It is noticeable that the Gospel of Mark was much less edited in this way than the other Gospels, no doubt because there were hardly any Commentaries on Mark. Folio 274b (Fig. 3) shows the sections and table-numbers in the left-hand margin, and at the head of the page a liturgical direction to John 1: 29:– 'On the morrow of Epiphany at the Commemoration of John the Baptist' (7 January). The beginning of this Lesson is marked towards the bottom of the page. At John 1: 28 the main text has: 'This took place at Bethany beyond Jordan, where John was baptizing', but there is a note at the foot 'Another manuscript has "in Betharaba"', showing that the scribe had seen another manuscript with this rare reading. A number of witnesses have in their text or margin 'Bethabara', which is recommended by Origen, but rejected by modern criticism.

Another early minuscule, Egerton MS 2610, also has an interesting text in Mark. It was written in the tenth or eleventh century and consists of 296 small leaves and has miniatures of the four evangelists. We have already met this manuscript when we looked at the Lord's Prayer in Luke. In Mark it has a text related to the text-family called 'Caesarean'. Eusebius quotes from a text of this type in works he wrote at Caesarea in Palestine. This family includes the ninth-century Koridethi-codex (now at Tiflis) and the minuscules 1 and its 'family' and 13 and its 'family'. This text seems to be a conscious compromise between the text-family represented by Sinaiticus and Vaticanus, the so-called 'Neutral' text which was supposed to have

10 *Gospels showing scholia,* 10th cent.
Additional MS 11300, f.31. 7×4¾ins (178×121mm). Greg. 478

λόν μου πρὸ προσώπου σου· ὃς
ἑτοιμάσει τὴν ὁδόν σου ἔμπρο-

ρδ σθέν σου· ἀμὴν λέγω ὑμῖν· ὀ-
υκ ἐγήγερται ἐν γεννητοῖς γυναικῶν
μείζων Ἰωάννου τοῦ βαπτιστοῦ·
ὁ δὲ μικρότερος ἐν τῇ βασιλείᾳ
τῶν οὐρανῶν μείζων αὐτοῦ ἐστιν·

ρε ἀπὸ δὲ τῶν ἡμερῶν Ἰωάννου
τοῦ βαπτιστοῦ ἕως ἄρτι ἡ βασιλεία
τῶν οὐρανῶν βιάζεται, καὶ βια-
σταὶ ἁρπάζουσιν αὐτήν·

ρϛ πάντες γὰρ οἱ προφῆται καὶ ὁ νόμος,
ἕως Ἰωάννου προεφήτευσαν·
καὶ εἰ θέλετε δέξασθαι, αὐτός ἐστιν
Ἡλίας ὁ μέλλων ἔρχεσθαι· ὁ ἔχω
ὦτα ἀκούειν ἀκουέτω· Τ

ρζ τίνι δὲ ὁμοιώσω τὴν γενεὰν ταύ-
την· ὁμοία ἐστὶ παιδίοις ἐν ἀγο-
ραῖς καθημένοις, καὶ προσ-
φωνοῦντι τοῖς ἑτέροις αὐτῶν, καὶ
λέγουσιν· ηὐλήσαμεν ὑμῖν, καὶ
οὐκ ὠρχήσασθε· ἐθρηνήσαμεν
ὑμῖν, καὶ οὐκ ἐκόψασθε· ἦλθε
γὰρ Ἰωάννης μήτε ἐσθίων μήτε
πίνων, καὶ λέγουσιν δαιμόνιον
ἔχει· ἦλθεν ὁ υἱὸς τοῦ ἀνθρώπου ἐσθί-

been preserved uncorrupted from an early date, and the text-family represented by the Codex Bezae (D) and the old Latin Version, the 'Western' text, so called because many, but not all, of its witnesses come from the western half of the Roman Empire.

Additional MS 28815 (Gospels, Acts, Catholic Epistles and Paul's Letters to Romans, Corinthians and Galatians), now re-united with Egerton MS 3145 (Ephesians to Revelation), is a magnificent manuscript written in beautiful minuscules in the middle of the tenth century. The first half was bought by the British Museum in 1871. The second half was bought in 1864 in Janina in Greece for Angela Burdett-Coutts. She later gave it to Highgate School, which sold it to the British Museum in 1938. The Additional Manuscript contains 302 large leaves, and has a portrait of John, and two portraits of Luke, one at the beginning of his Gospel, seated as a scribe, and the other, at the beginning of Acts, standing in the pose of an ancient Greek philosopher. These fine portraits are not original to the manuscript, and were probably painted a little earlier. The page that is illustrated (f.135; Fig. 5) contains John 5: 33–47, and shows Sections 44 and 45 with their appropriate tables 3 and 10. We have already seen (p. 15) that this manuscript has marginal glosses. It is in fact well equipped with introductions and notes on Acts and the Epistles, especially the Epistle of James. The notes, written in the margin in an uncial script, are in some cases attributed to Origen, Ammonius or Severianus, whose commentaries were abstracted for this purpose. Old Testament quotations are identified: so the quotation at 1 Corinthians 2: 9 'What no eye has seen, nor ear heard' is attributed to the apocryphal Apocalypse of Elijah, although it does not appear in the surviving fragments of that work. There is a note on the inscription 'To the unknown god', which Paul referred to in his speech to the Council of the Areopagus in Athens (Acts 17: 23). The full text is given as 'To the gods of Asia and Europe and Africa, to the unknown and foreign god'.

We saw in Additional MS 28815 the typical series of marginal notes abstracted from full-scale commentaries. We now show (Fig. 11 Papyrus 2921) a page from a complete commentary on Psalms 20–44. This is the first page of a gathering. The number of the gathering (13) can be seen at the top left corner of the page, which contains Psalm 33: 6–7 and its commentary, each phrase of the biblical text being followed by an exposition of the phrase. There were at least 338 large and nearly square pages, arranged in codex-form. This book was written in the 5th or 6th century and is now scattered in several collections. It was discovered about

11 *Didymos, Commentary on Psalms* 20–44, 5th–6th cent.
Papyrus 2921 C. 10½×9½ins (267×241mm)

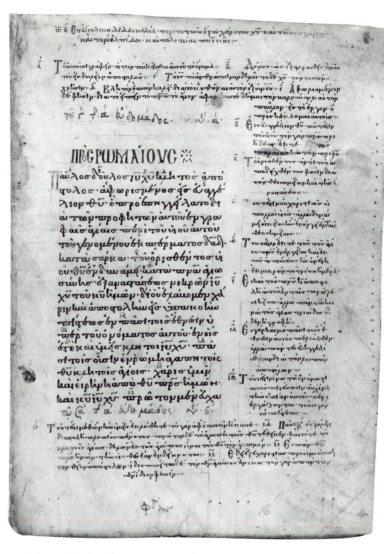

12 *Epistles of Paul with commentary*, 13th cent.
Additional MS 7142, f.9. 198 leaves, 12×9ins (305×229mm)

1940 during work at the Tourah quarry outside Cairo. It was a most important discovery of Christian books, and included many books by Origen and followers of his, such as Didymos. Didymos (*ca.* 314–*ca.* 398) became blind at the age of four, but overcame this handicap to achieve pre-eminence as a scholar and was made head of the Christian school of Catechumens at Alexandria. One of his pupils was Jerome, who asked him in 387 to write a commentary on Zechariah. This has survived only in one of the Tourah papyri, for when Origen's works were declared heretical two centuries after his death, the works of Didymos fell into oblivion with those of his master.

The layout of the papyrus commentary is inconvenient for reference, and a more suitable layout is shown in Fig. 12 (Additional MS 7142). This is a large thirteenth-century manuscript of the Epistles of Paul with commentary. This layout became the standard for Greek and Latin manuscripts of the middle ages. Additional MS 39601, which contains Revelation on 16 quarto leaves (the Acts and the Epistles now in a separate manuscript were once joined to it) has the same layout. The commentary is that of Andreas, Archbishop of Caesarea in Cappadocia. This manuscript, written in the eleventh century, was one of 200 manuscripts in Greek, Latin, Arabic and Syriac bequeathed in 1917 to the British Museum. They had been collected in the 1820s by Robert Curzon (d. 1873). Curzon published an account of his travels in *Visits to Monasteries in the Levant* in 1849, and it was reprinted many times. He acquired this particular manuscript from the Monastery of Caracalla on Mount Athos in Greece in 1837.

Lectionaries

W E HAVE SEEN HOW GOSPELS WERE written with indications to help find the right place for the daily Lesson. It was not long before a special book was designed with the Gospel-lessons arranged in order for the services of the church year, beginning with Easter. Additional MS 39602 (Fig. 13) is such a book, called a Gospel Lectionary. It contains the Lessons for each day from Easter to Pentecost, but only the Lessons for Saturdays and Sundays for the rest of the year. It also has the Lessons for the festivals and commemorations of the saints for the Byzantine civil year, beginning on 1st September. This large manuscript, which was also acquired by Curzon in 1837 from the Monastery of Caracalla, was written in the sloping uncials called 'Slavonic', not because the Slavs invented them, but because the newly-converted Slavs adopted them for the alphabet invented for their language by St Cyril and St Methodius, who converted the Slavs to Christianity. The colophon, or scribe's note at the end of the book, tells us that it was written in June of the year 980: 'The valuable and holy Gospel was written when Stephen was bishop of Kiskissa [near Kayseri in central Turkey], in the month of June, 8th indiction, in the Year of the World 6488 [i.e. AD 980] written by the hand of Niketas and T ( )'. There is a second note saying it was 'renewed' in AD 1049. This is not the earliest dated manuscript of the Bible; that honour is held by Additional MS 14512, which contains fifty palimpsest leaves of Isaiah in Syriac, dated AD 459/60. Syriac was an Aramaic dialect spoken in Syria, and it was here that the practice of signing and dating manuscripts started.

A slightly later lectionary has daily Gospels for every day of the church year beginning with Easter, and no Gospels for the saints' commemora-

13 *Lectionary in 'Slavonic' script with musical signs,* AD 980.
Additional MS 39602, f.111. 221 leaves, 12×8ins (305×203mm). Greg. *l* 181

ΑΥΤΟΙϹ ΕΚΕΙ ΚΑΙ ΟΥ
ΤΟϹ ΗΝ ΜΕΤΑ ΙΥ ΤΥ
ΝΑΖΩΡΑΙΟΥ ΚΑΙ
ΠΑΛΙΝ ΗΡΝΗϹΑΤΟ ΜΕ
ΘΟΡΚΟΥ ΟΤΙ ΟΥΚ ΟΙ
ΔΑ ΤΟΝ ΑΝΟΝ ΜΕΤΑ
ΜΙΚΡΟΝ ΔΕ ΠΡΟϹΕΛ
ΘΟΝΤΕϹ ΕΙΠΟΝ ΤΩ   οιεϲτω τεϲ
ΠΕΤΡΩ ΑΛΗΘΩϹ ΚΑΙ
ϹΥ ΕΞ ΑΥΤΩΝ ΕΙ ΚΑΙ
ΓΑΡ Η ΛΑΛΙΑ ϹΟΥ ΔΕΙ
ΛΟΝ ϹΕ ΠΟΙΕΙ ΤΟΤΕ
ΗΡΖΑΤΟ ΚΑΤΑΘΕΜΑ
ΤΙΖΕΙΝ ΚΑΙ ΟΜΝΥΕΙΝ
ΟΤΙ ΟΥΚ ΟΙΔΑ ΤΟΝ ΑΝΟΝ
ΚΑΙ ΕΥΘΕΩϹ ΑΛΕΚΤωρ
ΕΦΩΝΗϹΕΝ ΚΑΙ Ε
ΜΝΗϹΘΗ Ο ΠΕΤΡΟϹ
ΤΟΥ ΡΗΜΑΤΟϹ ΙΥ ΕΙ
ΡΗΚΟΤΟϹ ΑΥΤΩ ΟΤΙ
ΠΡΙΝ ΑΛΕΚΤΩΡΑ ΦΩ
ΝΗϹΑΙ ΤΡΙϹ ΑΠΑΡΝΗ

ϹΗ ΜΕ ΚΑΙ ΕΖΕΛΘΩΝ
ΕΖΩ ΕΚΛΑΥϹΕΝ ΠΙ
ΚΡΩϹ ΠΡΩΙΑϹ ΔΕ
ΓΕΝΟΜΕΝΗϹ ϹΥΜΒΟΥ
ΛΙΟΝ ΕΛΑΒΟΝ ΠΑΝΤΕϹ
ΟΙ ΑΡΧΙΕΡΕΙϹ ΚΑΙ ΥΠΡΕϹ
ΒΥΤΕΡΟΙ ΤΟΥ ΛΑΟΥ
ΚΑΤΑ ΤΟΥ ΙΥ ΩϹΤΕ
ΘΑΝΑΤΩϹΑΙ ΑΥΤΟΝ
ΚΑΙ ΔΙϹΑΝΤΕϹ ΑΠΗ
ΓΑΓΟΝ ΚΑΙ ΠΑΡΕΔΩ
ΚΑΝ ΑΥΤΟΝ ΠΟΝΤΙ
Ω ΠΙΛΑΤΩ ΤΩ ΗΓΕ
ΜΩΝΗ : -

ΕΥΑΓΓΕ Τ ΠΑΤΑ ΚΥ ΤΟΥ
ΑΜΗΝ ΙΧΥ ΕΚ ΚΑΙ ΙΩΑΝΝΗ

ΕΙΠΕΝ Ο ΚϹ ΤΟΙϹ ΕΑΥ
ΤΟΥ ΜΑΘΗΤΑΙϹ ΝΥ
Ε ΔΟΖΑϹΘΗ Ο ΥϹ ΤΟΥ
ΑΝΟΥ ΚΑΙ Ο ΘϹ ΕΔΟ

tions. It is Additional MS 39603, written in the 11th century (PLATE I). It is a large and magnificent manuscript with the text written in the shape of a cross on every page (only two other Byzantine manuscripts like this are known), in red ink throughout, and the first two pages over-written in gold, with fine decorative initials in the corners. It belonged to the Monastery of the Pantocrator on Mount Athos and was shown on feast days with the relics of the saints. During the Greek War of Independence it was transferred to the Monastery of Xenophon, from which Curzon bought it in 1837.

Another manuscript acquired by Curzon, this time in 1834 from the Monastery of St Sabba in Jerusalem, is Additional MS 39585, which contains Genesis to Ruth, written in the 11th century. Some 30 leaves have been lost from the original manuscript, and the gap has been filled in the 13th century, but in disorder, as if the manuscript which the scribe was copying from had been misbound. The later scribe had to squeeze the last pages of his new section to fit the text in. This manuscript contains 240 leaves of medium size. At the end of the manuscript the scribe has written in red: 'Readers, pray to the Lord for the writer, George, a sinful monk', and somebody has written below in black 'Completely checked'.

The Bible in the Royal collection, Royal MS 1 D. ii, which we quoted as reading 'handfuls' at 1 Kings 20: 10 (see p. 9), is a large 13th-century manuscript containing Ruth, 1–2 Samuel, 1–2 Kings, 1–2 Chronicles, Ezra-Nehemiah, Esther, 1–3 Maccabees, Esther (a different version), and half of Isaiah, as well as extracts from several other books. Another 13th-century manuscript in Rome has two Esthers like this one. One of the versions of Esther is the usual Septuagint text; the other is connected with Syria, and is supposed to be the work of Lucian of Antioch. Certainly Lucian is known to have been working on a translation or revision of the Bible. The manuscript, which was apparently once part of a complete Old Testament, is mostly written in two columns, but 32 leaves are written in three columns, which suggests that that particular section was copied from a very ancient manuscript, perhaps as old as the Codex Vaticanus, which is written in three columns.

The British Library has more Psalters (copies of the Psalms) than any other book of the Greek Old Testament, and Harley MS 5786 is a particularly interesting one. It is written in Greek, Latin and Arabic, and probably dated 1153. The date is rubbed and hard to read. There is only one place where this beautiful tri-lingual Psalter would be needed at that time, Sicily under the Normans. In Palermo a triumphant fusion of these three cultures can be seen and admired.

It seems appropriate to end this book with a look at an illuminated Psalter. The Psalter enjoyed a popularity second only to the Gospels, and luxury copies of both Psalter and Gospels were illuminated. The illuminated Gospels usually had portraits of the four evangelists and head-pieces to each of the four Gospels, but some illuminated Psalters had a frontispiece and a series of pictures in the margin, illustrating the text either allegorically or with a literalism worthy of Aquila himself, or else illustrating an event in the history of the church, such as the dispute over icons. The Theodore Psalter, for example, which was written in Constantinople in 1066, has, against Psalm 12: 3 'May the Lord cut off all flattering lips, the tongue that makes great boasts', a picture of an angel pulling out the boaster's tongue with a pair of tongs (PLATE VII). However, we avoid such a grisly scene and admire instead the frontispiece of the tiny tenth-century Psalter that belonged to the Western Baptist College in Bristol, which shows David and his musicians at court (Additional MS 40731, f.7b, PLATE IV).

We have seen that the study of ancient Bibles is a means of getting as close as we can to the original words, and also to watch the changes that reflected the views of the people who used it in successive centuries. The Bristol Psalter reminds us that the illumination in Bibles is a part of the history of art, and if we look at Bibles as products of technology we can learn something about the history of the technique of making books. In all these fields there is more than enough work still to be done.

Aland, K. and B., *The Text of the New Testament*, translated by E. F. Rhodes, Grand Rapids and Leiden, 1987.

Edwards, E., *Memoirs of Libraries*, vol. i, pp. 415–534, London, 1859 *Encyclopaedia Britannica*

Finegan, J., *Encountering New Testament Manuscripts*, Grand Rapids, 1974; London, 1975

Kenyon, F. G., *The Story of the Bible*, 2nd ed. with supplementary chapter by B. M. G. Reardon, London, 1964

Kenyon, F. G., *Our Bible and the Ancient Manuscripts*, revised by A. W. Adams, London, 1958

Kenyon, F. G., *The Text of the Greek Bible*, 3rd ed. revised and augmented by A. W. Adams, London, 1975

Metzger, B. M., *The Text of the New Testament*, 2nd ed. Oxford, 1968; 3rd ed. 1992

Miller, E., *That Noble Cabinet*, London, 1973

Milne, H. J. M. and Skeat, T. C., *Scribes and Correctors of the Codex Sinaiticus*, London, 1938

Würthwein, E., *The Text of the Old Testament*, translated by E. F. Rhodes, 1979

Plate VII *Theodore Psalter*, 1066. Add. MS 19352, f.11b